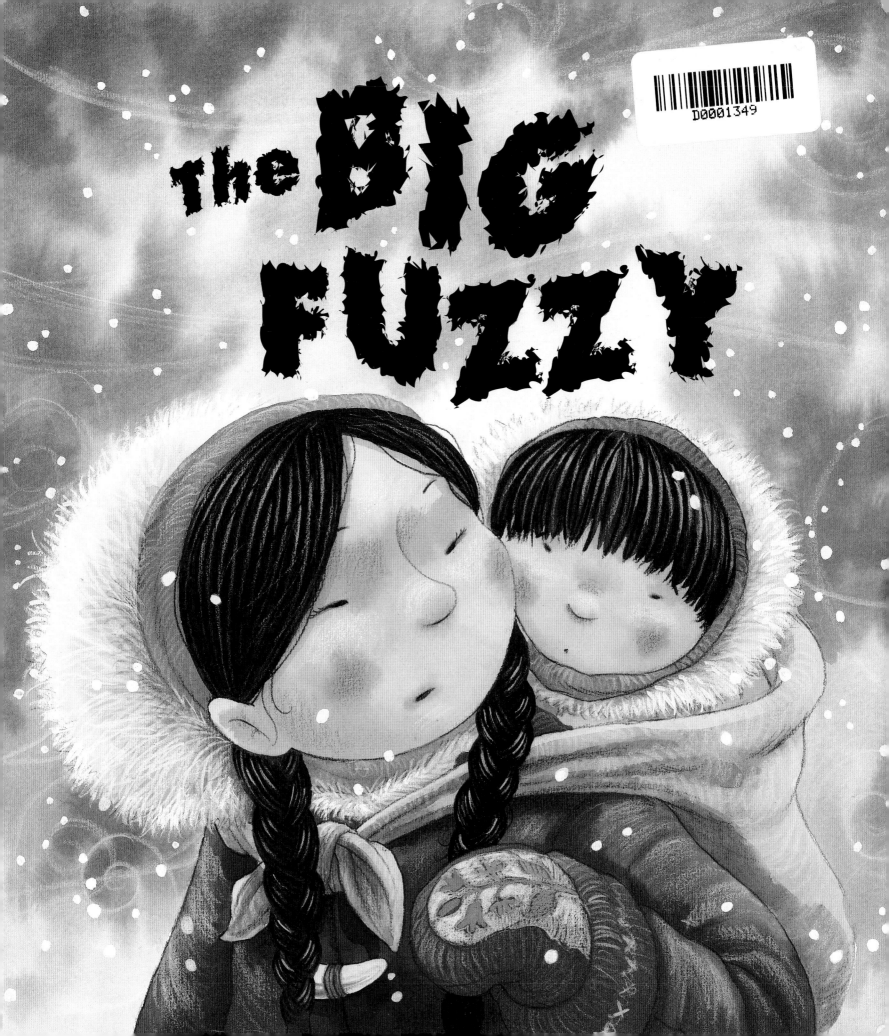

the BIG FUZZY

Copyright © QEB Publishing, Inc. 2007

First published in the United States by
QEB Publishing, Inc.
3 Wrigley, Suite A
Irvine, CA 92618

Reprinted in 2009

www.qeb-publishing.com

A CIP record for this book is available from the Library of
Congress.

ISBN 978-1-59566-875-2

Written by Caroline Castle
Edited by Clare Weaver
Designed by Alix Wood
Illustrated by Daniel Howarth

Publisher Steve Evans
Creative Director Zeta Davies
Senior Editor Hannah Ray

Printed and bound in China

the BIG FUZZY

Caroline Castle

Illustrated by Daniel Howarth

QEB Publishing

This is a story that happened long ago in a faraway land covered in snow. The land was called Greenland and still is today.

One **cold**, **cold** morning,

a domed shape rose out of the mist.

It was a little house made of ice! An **IGLOO**!

Someone was coming out the door.
It was Little Sira with her baby
brother Ivik strapped to her back.

Little Sira's mother was sick and couldn't get out of bed. Sira had to go out to catch some fish for supper or the family would go hungry.

"Be safe, brave Little Sira," called her mom. "And watch out for polar bears."

But as they set off, someone saw them go. Someone **big** and **white** and **fearsome**.

Oh, it was so very cold. But Little Sira was wrapped up warm as a winter fire. She made her way slowly through the snow until she came to a good place to fish.

Little Sira dug a hole in the ice and sank her line and hook. The sun was bright in the sky, and baby Ivik was sleeping.

But someone was watching. Someone big and **white** and *fearsome*.

Very soon, Little Sira caught her first fish!

But someone big and white and fearsome was creeping up behind her.

Someone big and white and fearsome... and hungry.

Baby Ivik woke up. "Big Fuzzy!" he laughed at the huge, furry face.

"Here," he said, "fishy?"

The big, white creature was so surprised that he took the fish and gobbled it up.

Little Sira caught another fish, and another.

"Fishies for Fuzzy!" laughed Ivik.

The big, furry creature gobbled them all up, bones and all.

The sky grew darker.
Little Sira heard the wind howl.
It whipped up the snow and whistled
around her ears. She knew it would
soon turn into a blizzard. It was time
to pack up the fish and go home.

But when she turned around, all
the fish were gone—every one!

"Naughty Ivik!"

cried Little Sira.
She was very cross.

But how could her little brother have eaten
all those fish? He was much too small.
Perhaps a seal came by and took them?
Now there was nothing for the family to eat.

"Big Fuzzy,"
said Ivik.

Whoooo! Whoooo!
howled the wind.
The sky grew darker
still. Fish or no fish,
Little Sira knew they
must go at once,
while they could still
see the way home.

So, Little Sira and
baby Ivik set off
into the blustery
evening. But the
wind roared like
thunder and blew
snow into their
faces. Sira couldn't
see the way.

Very soon,
Little Sira
and baby
Ivik were
both lost.

The nighttime fell like a thick, dark blanket.

And someone was following them. Someone **big** and **white** and **fearsome**.

Little Sira saw the shadow of a huge creature behind her. "Oh, something is coming," she cried out.

"Something **huge** and **fearsome!**"

"Big Fuzzy!"
cried Ivik.

Little Sira ran as fast as she could, but the snow was thick and she was tired. Ivik felt heavy, like a big sack of potatoes tied to her back.

Soon, she found herself by an icy cave. "We can hide in here," she said. They were so tired that they fell asleep right away.

They didn't hear the big footsteps
thundering through the snow.
One, two, **three**...

Slowly, slowly, the big creature
crept inside. He opened up his
huge, strong arms, and...

...very carefully picked up Little Sira and Ivik and folded them into his warm chest.

Then he ran and ran as fast as he could, over the snowy hills and through the blustery blizzard, all the way back to the igloo.

Little Sira couldn't believe her eyes.
How did they get home?

And where did that
big fish come from?

Only baby Ivik guessed
the answer. "Big Fuzzy,"
he said happily.

Notes for Parents and Teachers

- Look at the front cover of the book together. Talk about the picture. Can the children guess what the book is going to be about? Read the title together.
- Now look at the pictures together without reading the words—what do the children think is happening?
- Read the story to the children. Build up the suspense and the excitement of what will happen next. Enjoy the rhythm of the words and the repetition of the phrase: "someone big and white and fearsome." Were the children right when they guessed what was happening? Discuss how else the story could have ended.
- Encourage the children to take turns reading the story aloud. Help them with any difficult words and remember to praise the children for their efforts in reading the book.
- Study a map of Greenland with the children and choose a place where Little Sira and Ivik might live. Talk about Greenland and what life in such a cold and snowy country would be like. Here are some points to discuss: Greenland is the largest island in the world. More than 80% of Greenland is covered in snow and ice. People who live there used to travel by sled. What other methods of transportation might be used today to travel over the snow and ice?

- Explain to the children that Little Sira and Ivik are Inuit, which means "the people." In Greenland, the Inuits speak Kalaallisut, or Greenlandic. Here are some Greenlandic words that relate to the story: Kamik = boot, qanik = falling snow, panik = daughter, aqqalu = girl's younger brother, nanoq qaqortoq = polar bear, siku = ice, eqaluk = fish, puisi = seal. Make labels of the words and encourage the children to say them.
- Ask the children to imagine what it would have been like to live with Little Sira and Ivik and without cars, electricity, or central heating!
- Help the children make a collage of a snowy landscape. Once the landscape is complete, the children can make individual drawings or paintings of the igloo and some of the the animals that might be seen in Greenland. For example; polar bear, reindeer, seal, and wolf. The drawings can be stuck onto the collage and labeled with the names of the animals to encourage word recognition.
- Little Sira and Ivik wore lots of clothes to keep themselves warm. These were made from animal skin and fur. Ask the children to think about what they would wear if they were visiting Little Sira and Ivik. They can draw pictures of themselves wrapped up in their warm clothes.